GUELPH

398.
8
MCN

Signs of the times through reimagined nursery rhymes a colection of light verse for adults

SIGNS OF THE TIMES

Through Reimagined Nursery Rhymes

A Collection of Light Verse for Adults

SIGNS OF THE TIMES

Through Reimagined Nursery Rhymes

A Collection of Light Verse for Adults

by

Colin McNairn

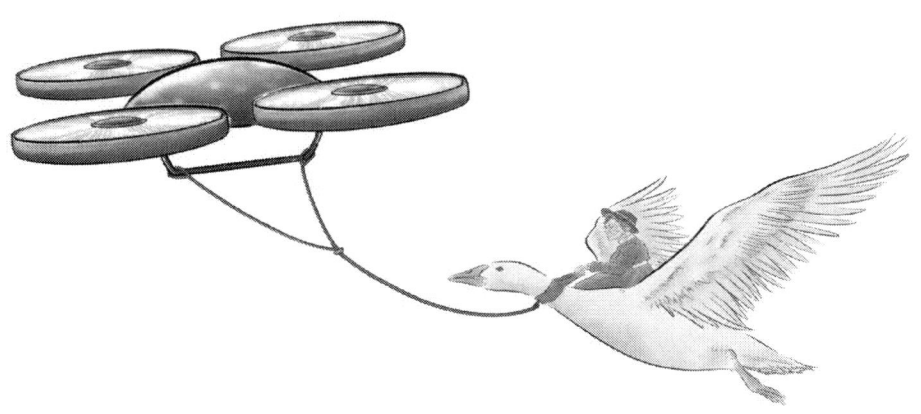

With Illustrations by Rosie Pittas

398.
8
MCN

© 2021 Colin McNairn. All rights reserved.
This material may not be reproduced in any form,
published, reprinted, recorded, performed, broadcast,
rewritten or redistributed without
the explicit permission of Colin McNairn.
All such actions are strictly prohibited by law.

Cover design by Shay Culligan

ISBN: 978-1-954353-69-5

Kelsay Books
502 South 1040 East, A-119
American Fork, Utah, 84003
Kelsaybooks.com

By the same author

In a Manner of Speaking:

*Phrases, Expressions and Proverbs
And How We Use and Misuse Them*

Sports Talk:

How It Has Penetrated Our Everyday Language

Table of Contents

Introduction

Politically Correct Language
    A Politically Corrected Nursery Rhyme — 17
    The Contested Terminology of Petting — 18

A Communications Barrier
    Simple Simon Converses with a Pieman, But It's All Greek to Simon — 19

On the Political Front
    The Ideal Political Platform — 21
    The Pinocchio Effect — 22
    A President Gets Fair Warning — 23
    A President Muses about Different Newses — 24

Risk Aversion
    Schoolyard Fun Be Damned — 25

The Legal System in Play
    A Fruitless Lawsuit — 26
    A Crooked Man Gets Bent into Shape — 27

Retributive Justice
    The Eggman Cometh — 28

Assisted Death
    Wealth Can Be Bad for Your Health — 29

Hanky-Panky
    A Proverbial Prescription for a Philanderer — 30

Odd Men and Odd Women Out
    My Son John Addresses Shoelessness with a Half Measure — 31
    Wee Willie Winkie: Small Is Susceptible — 32
    An Involuntary Celibate — 33
    The Polygamist: Seven Wives Proves to Be Too Many — 34
    This Lady Takes Twice as Long to Do Her Nails — 35

Gone off the Deep End
    A Rooster Crows about His Cockamamie Hen — 36

Trying to Get into the Swim of Things
    Aquatic Instructions   38
    Voyeurism Can Be a Washout   39
Making Sport of Sports
    Monday Morning Quarterbacks   40
    The Little Dutch Girl and Her Sporting Fans   41
Music to the Ears?
    Tom, the Scottish Piper's Son   42
Dialogue with Some Scots
    Faking It for Laughs   43
    Ancestry Says It All   44
The Mating Game
    Computer Dating Gets a Poor Rating   45
    A Floral Match-Up Fails to Blossom   48
    A Mixed Marriage, Believe It Or Not   49
The Sexual Revolution
    Women's Liberation Brings Men's Frustration   51
Sexual Harassment
    Sexual Harassment Is Out   52
    #MeToo   53
The Many Faces of Commerce
    Grooming in an Age of Recycling   54
    Blowing the Horn for Blue Movie Porn   55
    A McJob for a Working Slob   56
    Armchair Shopping   57
    An All-Consuming Business Investment Goes Sour   58
Medical Conditions
    Avoiding Contagion from a Tiger Toehold   59
    A Doctor Deterred by a Deluge   60
    Hay Fever Isn't Something to Sneeze at   61
    A Surgical Innovation Facilitates Relocation   62
    Double Disability Benefits   63
    A Polemic about the Pandemic   64

Household Hazards
    A Refrain about Blocking the Drain   65
The Technological Revolution
    When Technology Fails   66
    Trying to Avoid a Calculated Error   67
Food for Thought
    Bespoke Fruit Pies   68
    Getting Wind of a Pie-Eating King   69
    Is It Still Meat That We Should Eat?   70
Some Intoxicating Experiences
    A Grassy Knoll Takes Its Toll   71
    Distilling the Most Out of Life   72
    Brandy Outdistances Candy *or* Liquor Is Quicker   74
    The Rum-Tum-Tiddly Mouse   75
Petmania
    Mother Hubbard Goes Whole Hog for Her Unfortunate Dog   76
    Dog Gone: A Notice about a Lost Dog   78
    A Pet Lamb Is Afforded Cover from a Predatory World   79
Fantasias on an Animal Theme
    If Pigs Could Fly   81
    A Tale of a Missing Tail   82
Fowled–Up Fowl
    The Death of a Cocksure Rooster   83
    The Hen's Challenge: Getting Her Numbers Eggsact   85
    A Gander's Dander: What Gets It Up?   86
Other Birds of a Feather
    Name That Feathered Flock *or* Words for the Birds   87
    Little Tom Titmouse, A.K.A. Tittlemouse   88
    The Last Word from the Wise   89
Featherless Flocks
    The Sorry Fate of the Errant Sheep   90

Pest Control
    A Pretext for Getting a Ladybug to Bug Off   91
Off to See the City Sights
    Air or Ground When London Bound   92
    Coventry Gets More Exposure Than Banbury
        Cross   93
Contending with Adverse Weather
    Rain Fails to Deter the Frogs   94
    Coping with Global Warming: the Bare Essentials   95
Conservation through Adaptation
    A Lesson in How to Save the Endangered Camel
        One Cup at a Time   96
Recycling
    The Remains of Their Day Are Revitalized   97

Index of Traditional Nursery Rhymes   99

Introduction

In this book, I've taken the nursery rhymes of the fictional character, Mother Goose, and adapted them for adult consumption. The resulting "mature verses" generally take a humorous, sometimes cynical, look at the quirks and obsessions of modern life. Many of them play upon words or phrases that are part of our contemporary language, mainstream or colloquial.

Some of the mature verses are closely modelled on the underlying nursery rhyme and are best described as parodies. Others simply pick up on some of the words, phrases or lines of the original and go from there in a novel direction. The underlying nursery rhyme that's the trigger for each of the mature verses is reproduced, for ease of reference, following the mature verse.

There may be several versions of a nursery rhyme that have become popular over the years. When that is the case, I've selected one such version, in a more or less arbitrary fashion, as the launching pad for my take-off.

A Table of Contents, at the beginning of the book, lists the mature verses by title and the final Index directs the reader to the various original nursery rhymes, referred to by their initial lines.

Politically Correct Language

A Politically Corrected Nursery Rhyme

"Baa, baa sheep of whatever hue
Have you any wool you ewe?"
"Yes sir, madam or other, as the case may be,
I have three bags full as you can probably see;
One for the shepherd who's in charge of my flock,
One for the womyn (*sic*) in whom I put my stock,
And one for a dimensionally challenged boy:
And with these commitments I cannot toy,
So, regrettably, you're SOL,*
As I have no wool for you as well."

Baa, baa, black sheep,
Have you any wool?
Yes sir, yes sir,
Three bags full;
One for my master,
One for my dame,
And one for the little boy
That lives in our lane.

*This acronym is used here as short for "short on luck," and not for the alternative, crass phrase that was in common use in earlier times, which were marked by an abundance of unrestrained language.

The Contested Terminology of Petting

Dapple-gray is the name of my little pony,
My "animal companion," as PETA would say,
But I'd rather not have to pay palimony,
So she's my "pet," should we happen to split one day.

PETA tells me I'm my pet's "guardian,"
But should Dapple-gray ever be maimed,
I'd much prefer to be her "owner."
Property damage could then be claimed
And my insurer would pony up and give me a loaner.

I had a little pony,
His name was Dapple-gray,
I lent him to a lady,
To ride a mile away;
She whipped him, she slashed him,
She rode him through the mire;
I would not lend my pony now
For all the lady's hire.

A Communications Barrier

Simple Simon Converses with a Pieman, But It's All Greek to Simon

Simple Simon met a pieman,
Going to the fair.

Asked Simple Simon of the pieman,
 "What's the life of pie?"
"Depends how fast you eat it,"
Said the pieman in reply.

Asked Simple Simon of the pieman,
"Am I right that pie are squared?"
"Of course not," said the pieman.
"If you'd shape up, you'd know you erred."

Said Simple Simon to the pieman,
"I'd like to taste your ware."
"Put your money where your mouth is,"
Said the pieman, "That's what's square and fair."

So Simple Simon tendered to the pieman
All the small change that he could find.
But said the pieman to Simple Simon
"Bit coin isn't what I had in mind."

So Simon opted for a pie untried,
Offering the pieman three point one four (3.14),
Just what it was worth by his simple math,
But that price got him one slice and no more.

*Simple Simon met a pieman
Going to the fair;
Says Simple Simon to the pieman,
"Let me taste your ware."*

*Says the pieman to Simple Simon,
"Show me first your penny."
Says Simple Simon to the pieman,
"Indeed, I have not any."*

The remaining verses have been omitted.

On the Political Front

The Ideal Political Platform

If wishes were horses, beggars would ride.
If promises were made to be broken,
Politicians would be riding the tide.
They could comfortably promise the world
And have nothing whatsoever to do;
There'd be no need in deed to follow through.

If wishes were horses, beggars would ride.
If turnips were watches, I would wear one by my side.
And if "ifs" and "ands"
Were pots and pans,
There'd be no work for tinkers!

The Pinocchio Effect

Little Nancy Etticoat
In a white petticoat
Betrayed by her nose,
The more that she lies,
The longer it grows.

Too bad every fabricator
Doesn't have this indicator;
I wouldn't need my intuition
To recognize a politician.

Little Nancy Etticoat,
In a white petticoat,
And a red nose;
The longer she stands,
The shorter she grows.

Question: Who or what is she?
The Answer: A candle.

A President Gets Fair Warning

One little dickie bird
Sitting on a wall,
Known to be a tricky bird
Heading for a fall.
Fly away Richard!
Fly away Dick!
The Watergate has opened,
You'd better fly away quick,
Or you're sure to be sunk
By your cover-up trick.
Don't come back Richard!
Don't come back Dick!
You'll no longer have a perch
Atop the body politic.

Two little dickie birds
Sitting on a wall
One named Peter,
The other named Paul
Fly away Peter!
Fly away Paul!
Come back Peter!
Come back Paul!

A President Muses about Different Newses

What is the news of the day?
It's what Fox News has to say.
All the other main sources
Have, by now, run their courses.
It's a failing press, so SAD!
And the people, they've been had
By this enemy of state
That can never play it straight.

But it's certainly not too late
To expose the fourth estate
With its mostly biased views
As it generates fake news,
Ignoring alternate facts
In its partisan attacks.
For flawless news, just see my tweets,
Which trumpet my unrivalled feats.

"What is the news of the day,
Good neighbour, I pray?"
"They say the balloon
Is gone up to the moon!"

Risk Aversion

Schoolyard Fun Be Damned

Girls and boys come out to play
But not in the schoolyard, not to-day.

The principal hopes you're sufficiently cowed
By the posted warnings that play's not allowed.

Don't come with a whoop, don't come with a call,
Don't even bother to come here at all.

Should you climb a ladder or scaling wall,
There'd be serious risk of a major fall.

And on a weekend, such as to-day,
There's no insurance that's left in play.

So you'll just have to play in the street,
Dodging traffic, while fleet on your feet.

Girls and boys, come out to play,
The moon is shining as bright as day.
Leave your supper, and leave your sleep,
And come with your playfellows into the street.
Come with a whoop, come with a call,
Come with a good will or not at all.
Up the ladder and down the wall,
A halfpenny roll will serve us all.
You'll find milk, and I'll find flour,
And we'll have pudding in half an hour.

The Legal System in Play

A Fruitless Lawsuit

I had a little fruit tree, nothing would it bear.
Was it simply due to contaminated air?
An arborist was called to diagnose my tree.
And he found that dirty air was, indeed, the key.
So I sued every air polluter I could see,
Benefiting lawyers without a sou for me.

I had a little nut-tree, nothing would it bear
But a silver nutmeg and a golden pear;
The king of Spain's daughter came to visit me,
And all because of my little nut-tree.
I skipped over water, I danced over sea.
And all the birds in the air couldn't catch me.

A Crooked Man Gets Bent into Shape

There was a crooked man whose crimes were very vile.
He found a crooked lawyer to defend him in crooked style,
But the straight-up judge ruled with a heavy hammer,
Convicting him and sending him to the slammer,
Where, with the aid of the rack,
He was straightened out at a single crack.

There was a crooked man, and he went a crooked mile,
And found a crooked sixpence against a crooked stile,
He bought a crooked cat, which caught a crooked mouse,
And they all lived together in a little crooked house.

Retributive Justice

The Eggman Cometh

As I was going to sell my eggs
I met a man with two peg legs.
He cracked my eggs and roused my ire;
That's why I set both legs on fire.

He rose from the ashes later that night
At barely half of his previous height.
I'd made short work of that terrible cad,
Never again would he dare to break bad.

As I was going to sell my eggs
I met a man with bandy legs,
Bandy legs and crooked toes;
I tripped up his heels, and he fell on his nose.

Assisted Death

Wealth Can Be Bad for Your Health

My old man had all of the money
And I was the destitute sonny
But I moved up my ultimate role
As beneficiary of the whole.

I knew, from what people say,
That where there's a will, there's a way,
So it became an obsession
That I succeed through succession.

I know I committed a mortal sin
But it's the only way that I'd begin
To enjoy the old man's bounteous estate
Before it was spent and I was too late.

My little old man and I fell out;
I'll tell you what 'twas all about,—
I had money and he had none,
And that's the way the noise begun.

Hanky-Panky

A Proverbial Prescription for a Philanderer

Late to bed but early to rise,
And you'll have got up and went
Before her husband arrives,
Back from his night shift
In a dawning surprise,
And so you'll avoid
Your early demise.

Cocks crow in the morn
To tell us to rise,
And he who lies late
Will never be wise;

For early to bed
And early to rise,
Is the way to be healthy
And wealthy and wise.

Odd Men and Odd Women Out

My Son John Addresses Shoelessness with a Half Measure

My usually level-headed son, John,
Diddles around in sock feet forever and anon,
But when, for his shoelessness, he gets derided,
He dons one shoe and walks round lopsided.

Diddle, diddle, dumpling, my son John
Went to bed with his stockings on;
One shoe off, and one shoe on,
Diddle, diddle, dumpling, my son John.

Wee Willie Winkie: Small Is Susceptible

Poor old Wee Willie Winkie,
No bigger than your pinkie,
Ran through the city
And, more's the pity,
He was upended and trod under foot
And, in his own small way, was kaput.

Willie never cared a tot or tittle
That his dimensions were so little.
If only he had stretched or grew some,
His fate would not have been so gruesome.

Wee Willie Winkie
Runs through the town,
Upstairs and downstairs
In his nightgown,
Rapping at the window,
Crying through the lock,
"Are the children in their beds,
For now it's eight o'clock?"

Subsequent verses have been omitted.

An Involuntary Celibate

Little Tommy Tucker
Was such a luckless sucker!
When he sang for his supper,
He'd get one pat of butter.
When he cried in his beer,
No one else shed a tear.
With such a pitiable life,
He could never land a wife
And, not so strange to tell,
He lived as a lonely incel.

Little Tommy Tucker
Sings for his supper.
What shall he eat?
White bread and butter.
How will he cut it
Without e're a knife?
How will he be married
Without e'er a wife?

The Polygamist: Seven Wives Proves to Be Too Many

I met a man with seven wives,
A polygamist who stopped at seven
As that would match his crowns in heaven.
But when each amassed sundry sacks, cats and kits,
Stress from these earthly goods had him at the end of his wits.

As I was going to St. Ives,
I met a man with seven wives;
Every wife had seven sacks,
Every sack had seven cats,
Every cat had seven kits;
Kits, cats, sacks, and wives,
How many were there going to St. Ives?

<u>The Answer</u>: One.

This Lady Takes Twice as Long to Do Her Nails

Every lady in this land
Has five nails upon each hand
Except in the travelin' carny show
Where she's got ten nails on every hand,
Twice as many as the good Lord planned.

Every lady in this land
Has twenty nails, upon each hand
Five, and twenty on hands and feet:
All this is true, without deceit.

<u>Caveat</u>: Close attention to punctuation is required in order to make sense of this nursery rhyme.

Gone off the Deep End

A Rooster Crows about His Cockamamie Hen

Cock-a-doodle-doo!
My hen has a loosened screw
And doesn't know what to do;
She doesn't have a clue.

Cock-a-doodle-doo!
How will my hen get through?
Till someone finds a fix,
Her wit, by half, will have to do.

Cock-a-doodle-doo!
I thought of something new,
I found a filler to use as a fix,
But the caulk just wouldn't hold true.

Cock-a-doodle-doo!
We've got to tighten the screw.
I've found the perfect man for that,
He's a handy shrink at Bellevue.

Cock-a-doodle-doo!
My dame has lost her shoe;
My master's lost his fiddling stick,
And don't know what to do.

Cock-a-doodle-doo!
What is my dame to do?
Till master finds his fiddling stick,
She'll dance without her shoe.

Cock-a-doodle-doo!
My dame has found her shoe,
And master's found his fiddling stick,
Sing doodle-doodle-doo!

Cock-a-doodle-doo!
My dame will dance with you,
While master fiddles his fiddling stick
For dame and doodle-doo.

Trying to Get into the Swim of Things

Aquatic Instructions

"Can you teach me to swim?" asks my daughter.
"I can certainly tell you how you otter;
Just paddle like a dog
While kicking like a frog,
Then you'll take like a duck to the water."

"Mother, may I go out to swim?"
"Yes, my darling daughter.
Fold your clothes up neat and trim,
But don't go near the water."

Voyeurism Can Be a Washout

An itsy-bitsy bikini came frolicking down the beach
Out came an ogler, suspended in the shallows like a leech.
In came the noon tide and washed him clear away,
Drowning any chance at a flaunting display.

The itsy-bitsy spider climbed up the water spout,
Down came the rain and washed the spider out,
Out came the sun and dried up all the rain,
And the itsy-bitsy spider climbed up the spout again.

Making Sport of Sports

Monday Morning Quarterbacks

Sunday afternoon football on Monday morning re-played
By armchair QBs who give their team a failing grade,
But, with the help of their *post mortem*, it's sure to be true
That, next Sunday, the quarterback will know just what to do.

Friday night's dream, on Saturday told,
Is sure to come true, be it ever so old.

The Little Dutch Girl and Her Sporting Fans

I'm that little Dutch girl
Pictured on cleanser cans.
All the boys on the scrub team
Are among my greatest fans.

I am a pretty little Dutch girl,
As pretty as I can be, be, be,
And all the boys on the baseball team
Go crazy over me, me, me.

Subsequent verses have been omitted.

Music to the Ears?

Tom, the Scottish Piper's Son

Tom, the piper's nerve-wracked son,
Was forever on the run,
Trying his best to be long gone
Every time the pipes droned on.

Tom, Tom, the piper's son,
Stole a pig, and away did run,
The pig was eat,
And Tom was beat,
And Tom ran crying down the street.

Dialogue with Some Scots

Faking It for Laughs

A canny Scotsman once questioned me:
"How mony mickles mak a muckle?"
I answered in jest as I thought best:
"At least one, without counting the rest."
Truth is I didn't know a mickle from a muckle,
I just wanted to give the dour Scot a chuckle.

A man in the wilderness asked me,
How many strawberries grow in the sea?
I answered him, as I thought good,
As many as red herrings grow in the wood.

Ancestry Says It All

"A diller, a dollar, a miserly scholar!
Why are you so cheap?
You used to pay the posted price,
But now you claim it's too steep."

"It's due to my DNA,
Which marks me as a true Scot.
So now I behave as such,
Which makes me tighter than taut."

A diller, a dollar, a ten o'clock scholar!
What makes you come so soon?
You used to come at ten o'clock,
But now you come at noon.

The Mating Game

Computer Dating Gets a Poor Rating

"Oh, where have you been
Billy Boy, Billy Boy?
Oh, where have you been
Charming Billy?"
"I've been on a dating site,
Pursuing the marriage rite.
I've found my perfect match,
But she cannot leave her lover."

"Did she respond to your invite
Billy Boy, Billy Boy?
Did she respond to your invite
Charming Billy?"
"Yes, she said 'I accept'
But together we never slept,
For while she's a perfect match,
She cannot leave her lover."

"Can she make a cherry pie
Billy Boy, Billy Boy?
Can she make a cherry pie
Charming Billy?"
"Yes, she can make a cherry pie
But no matter 'cause it's by-the-by,
For I'm a perfect gastrosexual,
Yet even for me, she cannot leave her lover."

"How old is she
Billy Boy, Billy Boy?
How old is she
Charming Billy?"

"She's old enough to know better
And to break free if he'd let her,
But she's tied up by a pre-nup,
So she cannot leave her lover."

---

*"Oh, where have you been
Billy Boy, Billy Boy?
Oh, where have you been
Charming Billy?"
"I have been to seek a wife,
She's the joy of my life,
She's a young thing
And cannot leave her mother."*

*"Did she ask you to come in
Billy Boy, Billy Boy?"
Did she ask you to come in
Charming Billy?"
"Yes, she asked me to come in,
There's a dimple on her chin,
She's a young thing
And cannot leave her mother."*

*"Can she make a cherry pie
Billy Boy, Billy Boy?
Can she make a cherry pie
Charming Billy?"
"She can make a cherry pie
Quick as a cat can wink an eye,
She's a young thing
And cannot leave her mother."*

*"How old is she
Billy Boy, Billy Boy?
How old is she
Charming Billy?"
Three times six and four times seven,
Twenty-eight and eleven,
She's a young thing
And cannot leave her mother.*

A Floral Match-Up Fails to Blossom

A dusty miller sought common ground
With a cautious wallflower,
So he asked her to come round
And move into his bower.

But she resisted his plaintive plea:
"We are not at all suited
So I could never agree
To be fully uprooted."

"You're simply a dusty old miller
And I'm a fresh narcissus;
So it would be no thriller
For me to be your missus."

Margaret wrote a letter,
Sealed it with her finger,
Threw it in the dam
For the dusty miller.
Dusty was his coat,
Dusty was the siller,
Dusty was the kiss
I'd from the dusty miller.
If I had my pockets
Full of gold and siller,
I would give it all
To my dusty miller.

A Mixed Marriage, Believe It Or Not

A cat came fiddling out of a barn.
Believe that, you'll believe any yarn,
Even a church mouse marrying a bee
While the cool cat played fiddle-dee-dee,

A cat came fiddling out of a barn,
With a pair of bagpipes under her arm;
She could sing nothing but fiddle-dee-dee,

The mouse has married the bumblebee.
Pipe, cat; dance, mouse
We'll have a wedding at our good house.

The Sexual Revolution

Women's Liberation Brings Men's Frustration

I had a little chick, the prettiest ever seen,
She washed all my dishes and kept the whole house clean
Until drawn off the job by the wily Ms Lib,
Who must have seduced her with a little white fib.

I bought a dishwasher and robotic cleaner
But, still, the good old days seemed very much greener.
And I sure liked the cut of my little chick's jib
Before she succumbed to the wiles of Ms Lib.

I had a little hen, the prettiest ever seen,
She washed me the dishes, and kept the house clean:
She went to the mill to fetch me some flour,
She brought it home in less than an hour;
She baked me my bread, she brewed me my ale,
She sat by the fire and told many a fine tale.

Sexual Harassment

Sexual Harassment Is Out

If you're to be a true gentlemen,
As I suppose you'll want to be,
You will never harass women,
Singly or in quantity,
Yet you shouldn't come on
With an over friendly display,
For that could be taken
In quite the wrong way.

If you are to be a gentleman,
As I suppose you'll be,
You'll neither laugh nor smile,
For a tickling of the knee.

#MeToo

Georgie Porgie, known gadfly,
Kissed the girls and made them cry.
Had this happened since "Me Too"
He'd have been in deep doo-doo.

Georgie Porgie, pudding and pie
Kissed the girls and made them cry,
When the boys came out to play,
Georgie Porgie ran away.

The Many Faces of Commerce

Grooming in an Age of Recycling

Barber, barber, shave my bean,
I want to look like Mr. Clean
And give my hair to some bald coot
Who's always yearned to be hirsute.

Barber, barber, shave a pig.
How many hairs will make a wig?
Four and twenty; that's enough.
Give the barber a pinch of snuff.

Blowing the Horn for Blue Movie Porn

Little Boy Blue blows his own horn
To promote his cinematic porn.
Where's the censor to come down on this creep?
He's up in the projection booth, fast asleep.
"Should I wake him?" asks the usher at IMAX.
"Best not, for we'd all miss the climax."

Little Boy Blue, come blow your horn.
The sheep's in the meadow, the cow's in the corn.
Where is the boy that looks after the sheep?
"He's under the haycock, fast asleep."
Will you wake him? "No, not I;
For if I do, he'll be sure to cry."

A McJob for a Working Slob

See saw Margery Daw, as a last straw
She made a deal with the devil.
So she'll earn just minimum wage
'Cause she's not unionized and her job's entry level.

See Saw Margery Daw,
Jacky shall have a new master;
Jacky shall earn but a penny a day,
Because he can't work any faster.

Armchair Shopping

To your handy smartphone to buy a pork roast.
No shopper need leave home, that's Amazon's boast,
You simply must be there to welcome your roast,
No matter where you might live from coast to coast.
Is the supermarket now virtual toast?
Is its jig now up, should it give up the ghost?

To market, to market, to buy a fat pig;
Home again, home again, dancing a jig.
To market, to market, to buy a fat hog;
Home again, home again, jiggety-jog.

An All-Consuming Business Investment Goes Sour

Flush with loads of cash, little Miss Muffet
On advice from the great Warren Buffet
Invested in what she knew, curds and whey,
And she stuck with just that, never to stray.
But folks finally soured on curds one day
And whey alone she couldn't give away.
So she ate her final inventory,
Digesting a sad investment story.

Little Miss Muffet
Sat on a tuffet,
Eating her curds and whey;
Along came a spider
Who sat down beside her
And frightened Miss Muffet away.

Medical Conditions

Avoiding Contagion from a Tiger Toehold

Eeny, meeny, miney, moe,
Catch a tiger by the toe.
If that toe has nail fungus,
We don't want that cat among us,
So you'd better let him go,
Eeny, meeny, miney, moe.

Eeny, meeny, miney, moe,
Catch a tiger by the toe.
If he hollers, let him go,
Eeny. meeny. miney. moe.

A Doctor Deterred by a Deluge

Doc Martin went to Dumbarton
Got drenched in a bloody shower;
His hemophobia kicked in
And he never went there agin.

Doctor Foster went to Gloucester
In a shower of rain;
He stepped in a puddle,
Right up to his middle,
And never went there again.

Hay Fever Isn't Something to Sneeze at

A little boy went into a barn
Where hay fever overpowered him.
He sneezed away till the cows came home
But they couldn't abide the bedlam.

The cows raised a beef with the farmer,
Hoping at last the sneezing to quell.
But he failed to silence the boy,
No matter that the cows had raised hell.

A little boy went into a barn
And lay down on some hay.
An owl came out, and flew about,
And the little boy ran away.

A Surgical Innovation Facilitates Relocation

There was a housebound hunchback from Tobago
Who had a very bad case of lumbago
Till they put rebar up his spine
And his shape was so fine,
He headed straight up to San Diego.

There was an old man of Tobago
Who lived on rice, gruel, and sago,
Till much to his bliss,
His physician said this:
"To a leg, sir, of mutton, you may go."

Double Disability Benefits

Three blind mice! See how they run!
Erratically at best, causing the farmer's wife
To miss them with an initial blow from her carving knife.
But she left them as amputees, cutting off their tails with a second slice
And thus doubling the disability benefits of the, now tailless, blind mice.

Three blind mice! See, how they run!
They all ran after the farmer's wife,
Who cut off their tails with the carving knife!
Did you ever see such a thing in your life?
Three blind mice!

A Polemic about the Pandemic

Ding, dong, bell
Kat is in the well
Who put her in?
Little Doctor Fauci did,
After he'd made a futile bid
To get her to do as he asked
And go about properly masked.
So there she'd stay in quarantine
Until she got that new vaccine,
Or that's what the good doctor thought
Although it turns out he ought not,
For a human rights team pulled her out,
Setting her free to mingle about.
They never thought once, let alone twice,
About seeking scientific advice.
If they had just left well enough alone,
The virus might not have become full blown.

Ding, dong, bell,
Pussy's in the well.
Who put her in?
Little Johnny Green.
Who pulled her out?
Little Tommy Stout.
What a naughty boy was that,
To try to drown poor pussy cat,
Who never did him any harm,
And killed the mice
In his father's barn.

Household Hazards

A Refrain about Blocking the Drain

There's a ring around the bathtub.
How do you get rid of that stain?
Use a cleanser, give it a rub
Then wash it quickly down the drain.

But don't use a soft tissue,
For it could clog up the drain
And that would be a big issue
Should it flood the whole salle de bain.

If you had to call in a plumber
Because you'd ignored my advice,
That would be a real bummer,
For you'd end up soaked twice.

Ring around the rosie
A pocketful of posies
"A-tishoo! A-tishoo!
We all fall down.

The Technological Revolution

When Technology Fails

Twinkle, twinkle, little drone.
How I wonder where you've flown,
Aloft in the evening sky,
Your GPS gone awry.

Twinkle, twinkle, little drone.
Can you get home on your own
Unaided by a satellite
To guide you on your evening flight?

Twinkle, twinkle, little star,
How I wonder what you are.
Up above the world so high,
Like a diamond in the sky.
Twinkle, twinkle, little star,
How I wonder what you are.

Trying to Avoid a Calculated Error

Multiplication is vexation
Division is as bad,
But none of that bothers me
For now I've got an iPad,
Which can do the math for me
When it's not driving me mad.
But when my pad is on the fritz
And I attempt the math by hand,
I come off looking like a ditz
Who's cognitively undermanned.

Multiplication is vexation,
Division is as bad;
Rule of Three doth puzzle me,
And Practice drives me mad.

Food for Thought

Bespoke Fruit Pies

Our little Jack Horner
Was never forlorner
Than when roundly and squarely chastised
For plumbing the depths of fruit pies.

He would stick in his thumbs,
Pull out all of the plums,
Making the pies less plump
And causing consumers to grump.

Despite such caterwauling
Jack would find his true calling
In serving those who preferred plum-free pie,
And then he could cry: "What a plum-plumber am I!"

Little Jack Horner
Sat in a corner,
Eating his Christmas pie.
He put in his thumb,
And he pulled out a plum,
And said, "What a good boy am I!"

Getting Wind of a Pie-Eating King

Sing a song of twenty bucks
A mickey full of rye,
While two cans of navy beans
Were baked in a pie.

When the pie was eaten,
The musical fruit began to sing.
Now wasn't that a windy dish
To set before the king?

Sing a song of sixpence,
A pocket full of rye;
Four and twenty blackbirds
Baked in a pie;

When the pie was opened,
The birds began to sing;
Wasn't that a dainty dish
To set before the king?

The remaining two verses have been omitted.

Is It Still Meat That We Should Eat?

Jack Spratt would eat no fat,
His wife would eat no lean.
So both forsook the sins of the flesh
To join the vegetarian scene.

And so they got the benefit
Of the latest culinary feat,
And could complement their veggies
With a side of meatless meat,
Prompting wistful recall
Of what they used to eat.

Jack Spratt could eat no fat
His wife could eat no lean
And so between the two of them
They licked the platter clean.

Some Intoxicating Experiences

A Grassy Knoll Takes Its Toll

Jack and Jill went up the hill
To get a few tokes of grass.
Jack got high and strained his thigh,
Toppling him on his ... *gluteus maximus*.

Up Jack got and home did trot
As fast as he could limp.
He went to bed to clear his head
And Jill fairly jilted the gimpy wimp.

Jack and Jill went up the hill
To fetch a pail of water;
Jack fell down and broke his crown,
And Jill came tumbling after.

Up Jack got, and home did trot,
As fast as he could caper;
And went to bed and bound his head
With vinegar and brown paper.

Distilling the Most Out of Life

There was an old woman
Lived under a hill,
Made buckets galore
From her underground still.
A love of the moonshine
Is what keeps her there still,
As she drinks up the profits,
Never getting her fill.
And if God's willing
And the creek don't rise,
She'll keep on distilling
And getting her highs.

*There was an old woman
Lived under a hill;
And if she's not gone,
She lives there still.*

Brandy Outdistances Candy *or* Liquor Is Quicker

Jack Handy loved sugar candy
Until he got wind of brandy;
He bought some at a liquor store
And got high much faster than before.

Handy Spandy, Jack-a-dandy,
Loves plum-cake and sugar candy;
He bought some at a grocer's shop
And out he came, hop-hop-hop.

The Rum-Tum-Tiddly Mouse

Hickory, dickory, dock,
The soused mouse ran up the clock.
The clock struck thirteen,
The mouse ran down,
Thinking he'd run overtime.
Hickory, dickory, daiquiri.

Hickory, dickory, dock,
The mouse ran up the clock;
The clock struck one,
The mouse ran down;
Hickory, dickory, dock.

Petmania

Mother Hubbard Goes Whole Hog for Her Unfortunate Dog

Young Mother Hubbard
Went to the cupboard
To get her poor dog
An organic, gluten-free,
Hypoallergenic, anti-fungal,
Non-genimodified, CBD-infused,
Sugar-free dog treat.
But when she got there,
'Twas cause for despair;
Her supply was depleted,
So the dog went untreated.

To the pet wellness clinic
She went, dog treats to re-stock,
But when she finally got back,
The starving dog was in shock.

To the vet clinic she went
For fast emergency care.
But the dog died untreated
Before the vet could get there.

To see the mortician she went,
To get the dog's body treated,
But, worse luck, he too chanced to pass,
Before the job was completed.

The Moral: A dog left untreated will never have his day.

Old Mother Hubbard
Went to the cupboard
To get her poor dog a bone;
But when she came there
The cupboard was bare,
And so the poor dog had none.
She went to the baker's
To buy him some bread;
But when she came back
The poor dog was dead.
She went to the joiner's
To buy him a coffin;
But when she came back
The poor dog was laughing.

The remaining verses, describing more posthumous activities on the part of the dog, have been omitted.

Dog Gone: A Notice about a Lost Dog

Oh where, oh where has my little dog gone?
Oh where, or where has he fleed?
With his ears pinned back and his tail bobbed,
He looks like a brand new breed.

He's much like a modern designer dog
Which we used to call a mutt,
A creature we thought was a kind of dog
But we didn't know just what.

Should you find my peripatetic pet
Just wandering out and about,
My thanks and a hefty reward you'll get
For returning this odd dog out.

Oh where, oh where has my little dog gone?
Oh where, oh where can he be?
With his ears cut short and his tail cut long,
Oh where oh where can he be?

A Pet Lamb Is Afforded Cover from a Predatory World

Mary had a little lamb
Who got fleeced where'er he went;
He would fall for every scam
In the whole wide firmament.

So he stuck close to Mary
And she dressed him like a wild boar,
That way he seemed quite scary
And less fleeceable than before.

He followed her to school one day;
Alas, 'twas in a wool-free zone,
And his sad bleat gave him away
Due to its truly sheepish tone.

The teacher quickly cottoned on
And cut the lamb's school visit short,
Which silenced the lamb from then on,
Except for the odd boar-like snort.

Mary had a little lamb,
It's fleece was white as snow;
And everywhere that Mary went
The lamb was sure to go.

He followed her to school one day
Which was against the rule;
It made the children laugh and play,
To see a lamb at school.

And so the teacher turned him out,
But still he lingered near;
And waited patiently about
Till Mary did appear.

"What makes the lamb love Mary so?"
The eager children cry;
"Why, Mary loves the lamb, you know,"
The teacher did reply.

Fantasias on an Animal Theme

If Pigs Could Fly

Dickory, dickory dare
The pig flew up in the air.
Little chance of that I'd swear.

But if pigs could really fly,
There'd be fallout from the sky
That no skeptic could deny.

We're much better off the way things is,
For we're free to go about our biz
Without worrying if the pig's done his.

Dickory, dickory, dare,
The pig flew up in the air;
The man in brown soon brought him down,
Dickory, dickory, dare.

A Tale of a Missing Tail

I met a pushmi-pullyu on the trail
And asked; "Whatever happened to your tail?"
He replied from both ends in unison:
"Two heads are very much better than one
But, to attain a perfect symmetry,
One of those heads is where a tail should be,
Though the trouble is, to put it tersely,
I can go ahead but not reversely."

See, see! What shall I see?
A horse's head where his tail should be.

Fowled–Up Fowl

The Death of a Cocksure Rooster

Who killed the proud cock of the walk?
"I did," said the little red hen,
"And I'd do it all over again,
Egged on by the rest of the flock."

How did you kill that strutting cock?
"With a pea shooter," said the hen,
"I knocked him off his perch and then
He came down to earth like a rock."

Who saw him brought down from his roost?
"I did," said the fly on the wall,
"I witnessed his ultimate fall;
And knew, at that point, he was goosed."

Could we have foreseen this at all?
"Yes, of course," said the wise old owl,
"For it's specially true of fowl
That pride goeth before a fall."

Who would mourn the cock of the walk?
Answered the frog: "Some toady friends
Who would come round to make amends
For not calling out the proud cock."

Who killed Cock Robin?
"I," said the sparrow,
"With my little bow and arrow,
I killed Cock Robin,"

Who saw him die?
"I," said the fly,
"With my little eye,
I saw him die."

Who'll dig his grave?
"I," said the owl,
"With my spade and trowel
I'll dig his grave."

Who'll be chief mourner?
"I," said the dove,
"I mourn for my love,
I'll be chief mourner."

Several verses have been omitted.

The Hen's Challenge: Getting Her Numbers Eggsact

Higgledy piggledy, my brain-scrambled hen,
She lays eggs for gentlemen.
It's sometimes nine, sometimes eight;
She can never get her numbers straight.

Higgledy, piggledy, my black hen,
She lays eggs for gentlemen;
Sometimes nine, sometimes ten;
Higgledy, piggledy, my black hen.

A Gander's Dander: What Gets It Up?

Goosey, goosey, gander
What doth raise your dander?
Is it when an old man doesn't say his prayers
And, for lack of a savior, falls down the stairs
With a little assist if you get my gist?

Goosey, goosey, gander,
Whither dost thou wander?
Upstairs and downstairs
And in my lady's chamber.
There I met an old man
Who wouldn't say his prayers;
I took him by the left leg,
And threw him down the stairs.

Other Birds of a Feather

Name That Feathered Flock *or* Words for the Birds

Birds of a feather flock together,
Whether it's good or bad weather.
Like many of the groups in nature,
The flocks have their own nomenclature.
If they're crows, they're known as a murder
To every knowledgeable birder.
If they're wrens, they're best known as a chime,
A far cry from a serious crime.
If they're warblers, they're a confusion;
Passenger pigeons, an illusion.
Larks intone in an exultation,
Swans bemoan in a lamentation.
Vultures descend, *en masse,* in a wake
Then scavenge the dead for recycling's sake.

Birds of a feather flock together
And so will pigs and swine.
Rats and mice shall have their choices
And so will I have mine.

Little Tom Titmouse, A.K.A. Tittlemouse

Little Tom Titmouse lived in a birdhouse
As he was a tit rather than a mouse.
He defended his house, giving tit for tat,
And never turned another cheek after that.

Little Tommy Tittlemouse
Lived in a little house;
He caught fishes
In other men's ditches.

The Last Word from the Wise

A wise old owl sat in a tree
Grappling with loss of memory.
The less remembered, the more he was mute
Until, one day, he couldn't give a hoot.
So much for his great solomonic advice;
He's left us adrift in a fool's paradise.

A wise old owl lived in an oak
The more he saw the less he spoke.
The less he spoke the more he heard.
Why can't we all be like this wise old bird.

Featherless Flocks

The Sorry Fate of the Errant Sheep

Little Bo Peep failed to shepherd her sheep.
Left alone and perfectly free to roam,
To the wolves they were virtually thrown.
Those crafty beasts pulled wool over sheep's eyes,
Donning sheep's clothing by way of disguise,
Thus to surprise the sheep and do them in
By wolfing them down with a sheepish grin
And leaving only the tails behind them.

Little Bo-peep has lost her sheep,
And can't tell where to find them;
Leave them alone, and they'll come home,
And bring their tails behind them.
Little Bo-peep fell fast asleep,
And dreamt she heard them bleating;
But when she awoke, she found it a joke,
For they were still a-fleeting.

Subsequent verses have been omitted.

Pest Control

A Pretext for Getting a Ladybug to Bug Off

Ladybug, ladybug, beetle off home,
For your habitual habitation
Is engulfed in a huge conflagration.
Alas, your children have perished,
Along with all that you've cherished,
Except for quick and backward-thinking Ann,
Who went from the fire to the frying pan
Under which she found safety and shelter,
While all about her was helter skelter.
Now you've got to rescue poor little Ann,
So you'd best be off as fast as you can.

Ladybug, ladybug, fly away home,
Your house is on fire and your children all gone,
All except one and that's little Ann,
For she crept under the frying pan.

Off to See the City Sights

Air or Ground When London Bound

What a capital idea to head down
To take in the sights of London town.
They say the M1 is the way to go;
Trouble is, it can be terribly slow.
The alternative is, of course, shank's mare,
But that would take ages to get you there.
However, if you've that much time to spare,
You could take your chances and go by air.

See, saw, sacradown
What is the way to London town?
One foot up, the other foot down,
That is the way to London town.

Coventry Gets More Exposure Than Banbury Cross

Head to Coventry and, if you stay the course,
You'll see a young lady upon a white horse
Exposed to the world wherever she goes,
She's Lady Godiva, whom everyone knows.

Should you head to Banbury Cross instead,
There'd be nothing at all to turn your head,
Just a garish old lady upon a white horse,
Which isn't out of the ordinary course.

Ride a cock-horse to Banbury Cross,
To see an old lady upon a white horse;
Rings on her fingers, and bells on her toes,
And so she makes music wherever she goes.

Contending with Adverse Weather

Rain Fails to Deter the Frogs

It's raining, raining cats and dogs
But that doesn't bother the frogs,
The flies are about despite open skies
And, for frogs, time's fun when you're having flies.

It's raining and we're all soaking
But the happy frogs are croaking,
Likewise an old man who went to bed,
Bumped his head and, next morning, woke up dead.

It's raining; it's pouring.
The old man is snoring.
He went to bed and he bumped his head,
And couldn't get up in the morning.

Coping with Global Warming: the Bare Essentials

Whether the weather is hot,
We shall weather the weather,
For we're in it together
And we'll just do what we ought.

We'll walk around scantily clad
And adapt when it's hot
By not wearing a lot,
For clothing's no more than a fad.

Whether the weather be fine,
Or whether the weather be not,
Whether the weather be cold,
Or whether the weather be hot,
We'll weather the weather
Whatever the weather,
Whether we like it or not!

Conservation through Adaptation

A Lesson in How to Save the Endangered Camel One Cup at a Time

It's the straw that broke the camel's back.
Had baby used a sippy cup, the camel would still be intact.

Three straws on a staff
Would make a baby cry and laugh.

Recycling

The Remains of Their Day Are Revitalized

The London Bridge was falling
And had to be taken down,
But then was reassembled
In an Arizona town.

The Queen Mary was decrepit
And couldn't set sail any more,
But was reborn as a hotel
On the California shore.

Who could've ever imagined
That this iconic British pair,
Once thought to have succumbed,
Could spring to life elsewhere.

London Bridge is falling down,
Falling down, falling down,
London Bridge is falling down,
My fair Lady.

The many remaining verses have been omitted; they deal principally with the ways in which the bridge could be built up again and the various shortcomings of those approaches.

Index of Traditional Nursery Rhymes

A cat came fiddling out of a barn, 49
A diller, a dollar, a ten o'clock scholar, 44
A little boy went into a barn, 61
A man in the wilderness asked me, page 43
A wise old owl lived in an oak, page 89
As I was going to St. Ives, I met a man with seven wives, 34
As I was going to sell my eggs, I met a man with bandy legs, 28
Baa, baa, black sheep have you any wool, 17
Barber, barber, shave a pig, 54
Birds of a feather flock together, 87
Cock-a-doodle-doo! My dame has lost her shoe, 36
Cocks crow in the morn, 30
Dickory, dickory, dare, the pig flew up in the air, 81
Diddle, diddle, dumpling, my son John, 31
Ding, dong, bell, pussy's in the well, 64
Doctor Foster went to Gloucester, 60
Eeny, meeny, miney, moe, catch a tiger by the toe, 59
Every lady in this land has twenty nails, 35
Friday night's dream on Saturday told, 40
Georgie Porgie pudding and pie, 53
Girls and boys come out to play, 25
Goosey, goosey, gander, whither dost thou wander? 86
Handy-Spandy, Jack-a Dandy, 74
Hickory, dickory, dock, 75
Higgledy piggledy, my black hen, 85
I am a pretty little Dutch girl, 41
I had a little hen, the prettiest ever seen, 51
I had a little nut tree, nothing would it bear, 26
I had a little pony, his name was Dapple-gray, 18
If wishes were horses, beggars would ride, 21
If you are to be a gentleman, as I suppose you'll be, 52
It's raining, it's pouring, 94

Jack and Jill went up the hill, 71
Jack Spratt could eat no fat, 70
Ladybug, ladybug, fly away home, 91
Little Bo-peep has lost her sheep, 90
Little Boy Blue come blow your horn, 55
Little Jack Horner sat in a corner, 68
Little Miss Muffet sat on a tuffet, 58
Little Nancy Etticoat in a white petticoat, 22
Little Tom Tittlemouse lived in a little house, 88
Little Tommy Tucker sings for his supper, 33
London Bridge is falling down, 97
Margaret wrote a letter, 48
Mary had a little lamb, 79
Mother, may I go out to swim, 38
Multiplication is vexation, 67
My little old man and I fell out, 29
Oh, where have you been, Billy Boy? 46
Oh where, oh where, has my little dog gone? 78
Old Mother Hubbard went to the cupboard, 77
Ride a cock-horse to Banbury Cross, 93
Ring around the rosie, 65
See Saw Margery Daw, 56
See, saw, sacradown, what is the way to London town? 92
See, see. What shall I see? 82
Simple Simon met a pieman, 21
Sing a song of sixpence, 69
The itsy-bitsy spider climbed up the water spout, 39
There was a crooked man, 27
There was an old man of Tobago, 62
There was an old woman lived under a hill, 73
Three straws on a staff, 96
To market, to market, to buy a fat pig, 57
Tom, Tom, the piper's son, 42

Three blind mice! See how they run! 63
Twinkle, twinkle, little star, 66
Two little dickie birds sitting on a wall, 23
Wee Willie Winkie runs through the town, 32
What is the news of the day, 24
Whether the weather be fine, 95
Who killed Cock Robin? 83

Manufactured by Amazon.ca
Bolton, ON